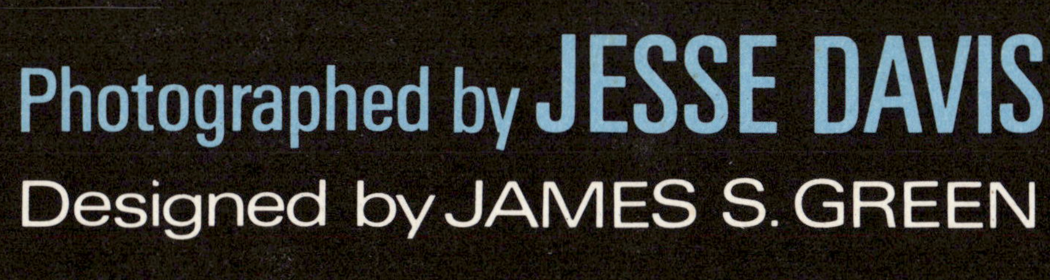

CONTENTS

Published by IPC Magazines Ltd., Fleetway House,
Farringdon Street, London, England. Sole Agents for
Australia and New Zealand: Gordon and Gotch Ltd;
South Africa: Central News Agency Ltd; Rhodesia
and Zambia: Kingstons Ltd. Printing and binding by
Istituto Italiano d'Arti Grafiche—Bergamo.

PRICE
80p

The *Overture* cast giving an
evening at the ballet a cheerful
start. On the far right are
Paul Clarke and Diana Vere.

A BALLET CALLED OVERTURE

Why shouldn't an evening at the ballet start off with fun and high spirits? Of course, there are always some serious folk who want all ballet to be sober stuff, beautiful to look at, but without the suspicion of a smile anywhere.

What a curious idea! Ballet is a popular art and everyone likes a laugh or a smile now and then. That was what the Royal Ballet rightly thought when the Company presented *Overture* for the first time at the Theatre Royal, Norwich, in February 1971.

The choreographer—the man who "composed" the steps and staged the lighthearted work—was Joe Layton, the designer was John Conklin, and the music that was used was Leonard Bernstein's overture to his musical show, *Candide*, not as well known as his *West Side Story* music, but as sparkling as *West Side Story* was dramatic.

There's not a real story to *Overture*. It gives five dancers a chance to shine and perform some very energetic movements, leaps and twirls—they have a ball in fact!

They appear dragging on an old cart full of junk, then dress up in old hats and anything else they can find to hand—and they find plenty!

For a while they cavort around, entertaining themselves and the audience, but then the moment comes for them to do a spot of advertising!

No, they don't go in for advertising washing-up powder or cigars or breakfast cereals—instead they advertise the ballets that are to follow during the rest of the evening!

Being ballet dancers, they don't shout their wares. Instead, they present the titles of the other ballets that particular evening, written in bold letters on strips of rags and paper!

They are like a little circus troupe really, a small gathering of male and female clowns. They warm the audience up with their little "curtain-raiser". They warm themselves up as well, for when this ballet was in the repertoire of the Royal Ballet, all the dancers would be dancing in ballets later in the evening.

What a marvellous idea it was! Ballet tends to get more and more weighty as the years go by, and a brisk start like this makes everyone, dancers and audiences alike, ready for the more solid fare to come.

The cast let the audience know the ballets that are to follow *Overture* by means of strips of paper and rags!

Marion Tait, Royal Ballet dancer,
who also appears as our Cover Girl,
along with Diana Vere.

Grecian Revels

The Greeks are mad about dancing! Looking through this book you might suppose that they are not the only ones, and you would be right, but Greece, that most beautiful of countries, has perhaps the longest tradition of folk dancing in the world.

Most of these are naturally performed in traditional costumes. The most famous of these is called a foustanella, worn by Greek Guards in full dress and, as the photos show, by many dancers. This is the skirt or kilt, a white, pleated garment which, when stretched out, can measure up to 40 yards!

A graceful, happy dance for the men and women of the village.

A mixed line-up, always a popular feature of Greek dancing.

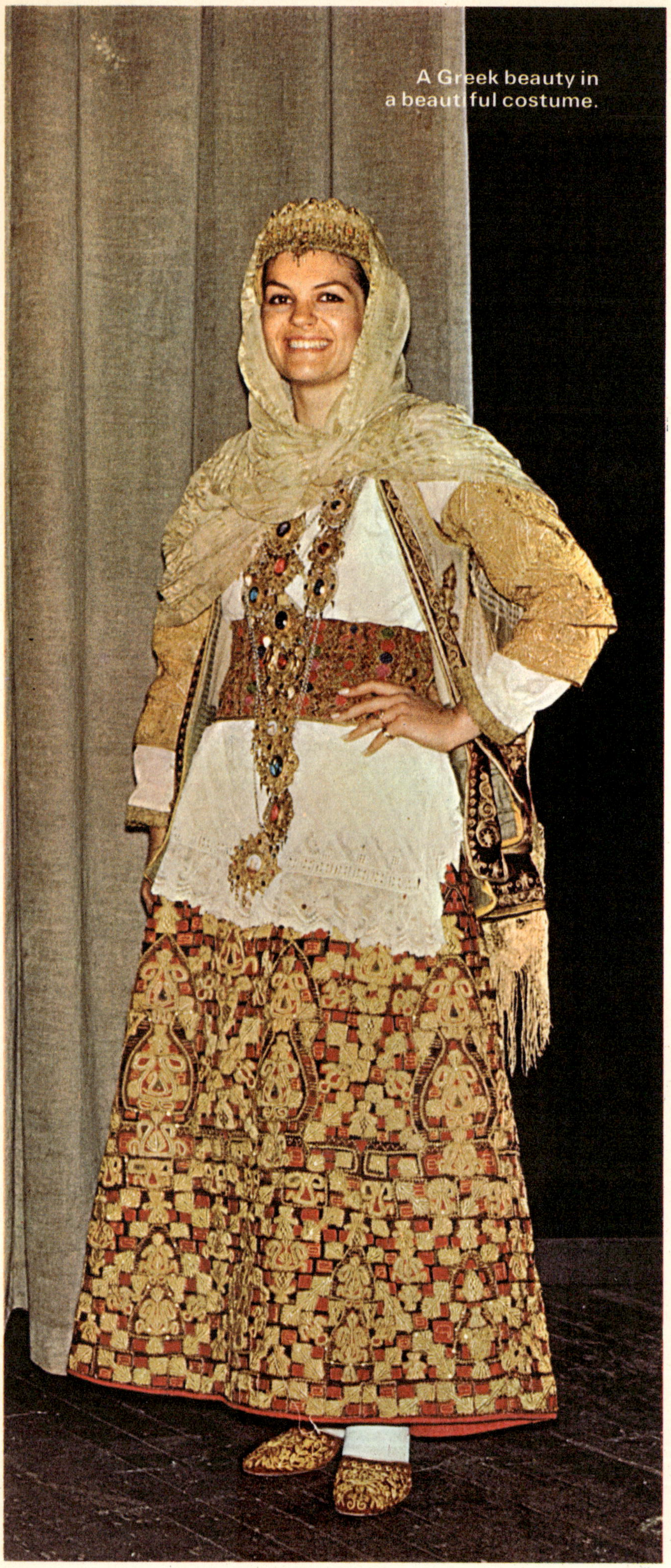

A Greek beauty in a beautiful costume.

The rest of the outfit—full-sleeved shirts, red shoes with big black pom-poms etc.—is traditional too, though costumes of men and women alike vary from district to district, as the dancing does.

Greece has a wonderful climate which encourages people to lead an open air life, full of gaiety, and Greek dancing naturally expresses this zest for life. You can find Turkish influence in some of the dances, for the Greeks were ruled by the Turks for hundreds of years before gaining their freedom.

Amazingly, some Greek dances are thought to have links with the dances of Ancient Greece which were being performed more than 2,000 years ago. This is not so easy to prove, but there is no doubt about the dances which date back to the times of Turkish rule. Some were invented by brave young freedom fighters, whose dances were circular and very military. Swords were used and, later, pistols were fired into the air, and these thrilling routines can still be seen in the Greece of the 1970s. Look out for stamps, leaps and cries of "Oppa", and if women are watching, the men seem to dance even better!

The men appear to be leaving, but don't worry! They'll be back.

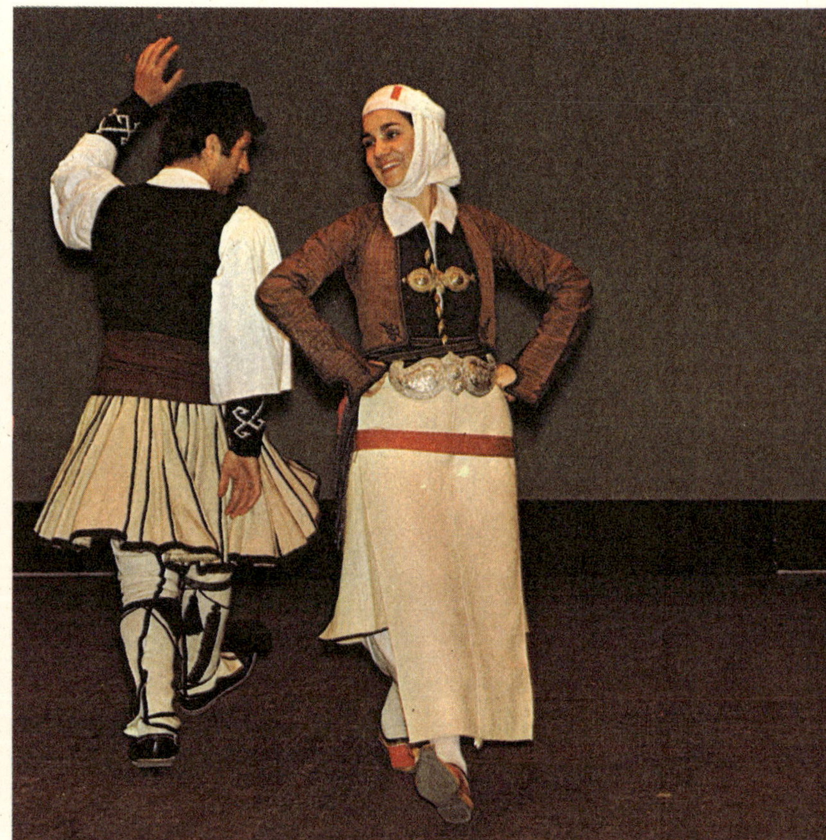

Music plays a big part in Greek
dancing, and sometimes (below)
the men get into masks.

Happy Grecian couples. They
can always be depended upon to
make audiences happy, too.

Another lovely line-up.
Another chance to applaud.

In fact, many Greek dances are circular. Some, like the Maiden's Dance at Megara, danced every Easter, are very simple, but wonderful to watch all the same. Others, especially those danced in the open by the Evzone guards, are wild gymnastic feats. One dancer has been seen to hold his beer mug by his lips and swallow his drink as he spun round and round. He even leapt in the air!

Of course, this sort of dancing could not be called beautiful, but what a thrill it is to watch! And there is always plenty of beauty as well. You could say that Greek dancing provides lots of beauty and plenty of action. Dance lovers can't ask for much more than that!

Thai Temple Dancers

Tap Will Make You Happy

Some of the pupils at the Dance Centre, London, with top tap teacher Gillian Gregory, in front (centre above) and watching happily (left).

*S*uddenly everybody's tap dancing! Well, not quite everyone, perhaps, but there's a big boom in tap, the biggest since the golden age between the world wars when Fred Astaire, Ginger Rogers and a host of other stars were dazzling us with their twinkling feet on the silver screen. Thanks to TV, today's tap fans can watch them as well.

The craze really took off around the time that Twiggy said she was going to learn tap for her film, The Boy Friend, and, we're happy to say there's no stopping it! It's not expensive, which helps. You can get shoes with the right metal plates on the heels and toes for from £3 to £5, and you can get the best lessons available for around 40p an hour. No one can say that tap is a rich person's hobby!

FORWARD TAP

A. Hold one leg slightly off ground behind the body.

B. Brush forward, striking floor with metal tap on sole of shoe.

C. Carry foot forward to raised position in front. Repeat action in reverse, creating a backward tap. Put them together and you have a shuffle.

Three basic tap steps demonstrated by Gillian Gregory

The Dance Centre, London, is the top tap spot. Our pictures were taken there and some of them show Gillian Gregory, Britain's leading tap teacher, putting the pupils through their paces.

Tap dancing is descended from the old time clog dances of the North of England, but its modern form was begun in the U.S.A. by Irish immigrants. The Negroes, those masters of rhythm, joined in the act, which was going strong about 100 years ago. In the 20s, 30s and 40s, hardly a star was to be found in musical films who could not tap, from the most famous child star of them all, Shirley Temple, to glamorous grannies! Let's hope that today's stars all follow their lead. Meanwhile, there's plenty of fun to be had for the rest of us.

HEEL TAP

The picture above shows the metal plates which "make" the sound, giving the dance its name.

A PICK-UP

D. Backward slap striking the floor with metal tap.

E. Heel placed on the floor.

F. Foot entirely off the ground.

TOE TAP

G. Raise foot off the ground.

H. Strike the floor sharply with tip of toe.

I. Raise again.
This move can be done in any position. It can also be done with heel tap by flexing the foot and striking with the heel.

TIP TOP TAP AT THE DANCE

CENTRE, LONDON

Pupils going happily through their
paces at the Centre. There's
Gillian Gregory demonstrating
a step out in front of them.
Note how cheerful everyone looks.
Tap does that to people!

Sleeping Beauty

The great composer, Tchaikovsky, was upset, and who could blame him? His new ballet, The Sleeping Beauty, had had a huge success on its opening night in Saint Petersburg (now Leningrad), the capital—and the dance capital—of Russia. He and the choreographer, Petipa, who had "composed" the dancers' steps, were the heroes of the hour. Yet all the Emperor of Russia, Tsar Nicholas II, could say when he was introduced to the composer was "Very nice"!

The music was far more than very nice —it was sheer magic, as generations of ballet lovers have discovered down the years. The Sleeping Beauty is just about the most popular classic ballet of all. "Very nice" indeed!

At her birthday party, Princess Aurora pricks her finger and falls to the ground. The threat of the Bad Fairy has come true, even though Aurora is only asleep.

The story of the ballet follows the old fairy story fairly closely, beginning on the christening day of Princess Aurora. In a great ceremony, seven fairies come to bring good fortune on the baby girl, but an eighth fairy arrives, as bad as the others are good, who says that the poor Princess will prick her finger one day and die. The Lilac Fairy manages to alter the curse a little—Aurora will not die, but will fall into a deep sleep, and one day she will be awakened by a kiss, bestowed by a king's son.

When the courtiers are
not asleep, they are full of
grace and life !

Which, as everyone knows, is what happens! Except that not only Aurora goes to sleep but everyone else in the Palace as well, to be awakened in due course by that prince of princes, Prince Charming.

The ballet follows these adventures closely, including the Prince's efforts to get to the Princess, aided by the Lilac Fairy. And once he has kissed Aurora and everyone else wakes up as well, there is a wonderful surprise for Aurora — apart from meeting her dream lover, of course! All her favourite fairy tale characters appear to dance for her, Little Red Riding Hood, Puss-in-Boots and all the rest.

Naturally, the Prince and Princess fall in love instantly; naturally, her father is only too delighted; and naturally—we assume —the happy pair live lovingly ever after!

The Tsar was right, of course. The ballet is very nice! But he was being sarcastic. We suppose!

Princess Aurora and her Prince Charming are united for ever as the ballet ends.

Fast and Furious

Once they were some of the most famous and daring horsemen in the world. Their very name could strike terror into the hearts of their enemies. Their homeland was in the Ukraine, which forms part of Russia, and their name was—and is—the Cossacks.

For centuries they were peasant-soldiers, supreme men-of-war. As those who saw *War and Peace* will know, it was the Cossacks who turned Napoleon's retreat from Moscow in 1812 into a nightmare, as if the Russian winter was not bad enough. They tore down on his ragged army—what was left of it—and killed and killed.

What, readers may ask, has this to do with a book about dancing? The answer is simple: the Cossacks always were and still are superb dancers. When not on the warpath, they enjoyed themselves at home, and enjoyment for all Russians includes song and dance.

Being Cossacks, their dancing is on the vigorous side! No, that sounds far too tame! Their dancing is wild, abandoned, electrifying, superb, proud, violent—everything one would expect from a warrior race, and a bit more besides!

Like all Russians, their dancing includes wonderful leaping, and all-action spectacle with the emphasis on action. These are dancers who seem untamed, dancers in whom the blood of their ancestors runs like a raging torrent.

Readers of this book will not need to be told that dancing is a manly art as well as a female one. They will know that only strong men can possibly hope to succeed as ballet dancers. But few ballet dancers would claim to be as tough as Cossacks, few other men if it comes to that. The Cossacks have even withstood pressure to make them behave like other Russians. Not that they are not good patriots—they are—but they are Cossacks still.

Fortunately, the world can glimpse something of their splendour when their dancers leave Russia and tour abroad. An evening spent watching these ultra-lively, explosive warriors in action—for peaceful purposes—is an evening very well spent!

When the Cossacks are in full cry some members of their audiences must wonder if they are safe. Will these warrior-dancers erupt into the aisles and start behaving like their ancestors?

The Cossack way of life was not all war and action. They were—and are—family men as well as warriors, and so it is not surprising that their womenfolk take part in the dances as well as the men.

And very graceful they are too, looking as lovely in their traditional costumes as the men look stunning in their uniforms.

The only pity is that the Cossacks cannot bring their horses on to the stage, too. Such is their control, that they would undoubtedly manage them beautifully, even in a small space, but, life being what it is, people will have to make do with just about the most thrilling dancing to be seen in a month of Sundays!

Of course, we must not suggest that many other Russian dance troupes are not renowned for their thrilling dancing. They are! And their vigour is famous throughout the dance world, rightly. But the Cossacks are unique. Perhaps it is their past which helps them be so, perhaps their very name thrills audiences before they even begin to perform. Whatever it is, they are—there is no other word for it—sensational!

The Cossacks are not just warriors, dancers and horsemen. They are circus performers as well!

The picture above makes it seem as if Cossacks can actually fly! We are not saying that they cannot, for their versatility is incredible, but a closer look at the picture shows that the mighty man has leapt from the shoulders of his colleagues!

As horsemen, the Cossacks gained a reputation as high as Red Indians, who lived thousands of miles from the Russian Steppes. Without in any way running down Indian dancing, it must be stated that it was never in the Cossack class. But then, as we have seen, these Russian marvels are unique, second to none.

Perhaps some of them should be imported to all those countries where dancing is considered rather a sissy art. One glimpse of them would be enough to knock that stupid idea right out of the sneerers' heads for ever.

The flying Cossacks! Their
womenfolk expect them to take off
like rockets, and they expect their
wives and sweethearts to be graceful in
the extreme. A perfect combination.

Caribbean Jazz

Yes, we know that jazz was born in New Orleans, but West Indians have got rhythm in a big way, too! Tell a Trinidadian or a Jamaican or a Barbadian, or anyone from any of the colourful islands of the Caribbean that he should stick to Calypsos and steel bands and you would rightly get yourself into an argument. The chances are, though, that it would be friendly. After all, it's probably carnival time, and life's for living, not arguing!

Those jazzy rhythms get under your skin. You feel like smiling, as the dancers do in the pictures on this page and the next. It isn't carnival time every day, wages are low, times are hard, prospects are less than promising, so let's dance, Caribbean style!

If you happen to be in Trinidad, that includes everyone! Of course, you can see these dancers in a theatre or on television. They are the tops, the cream of the local talent, who are worth anybody's money. So if you see that they are playing down your way just step inside, sit yourself down, relax and enjoy yourself. If you can keep still, that is. If not, well, you may get asked to join in. If you happen to be in the Caribbean you won't get asked to join in the carnival—you're in it already, along with everyone else.

Carnivals aren't confined to the Caribbean or to New Orleans. One of the best is in Brazil. Try rolling down to Rio de Janiero for the most famous one in South America. But why not sample West Indian hospitality first? You'll find more than fun, for you'll notice that everybody in the big parade seems to be a born dancer. Seems? There's no doubt about it. In the islands they are born with rhythm!

The party's in full swing!
Caribbean rhythm, throbbing music,
smiling faces, flashing feet.
There's no carnival today, but
this could easily turn into
one. Meanwhile, let's enjoy
ourselves. Forget your
troubles, relax and join in!

BALKAN BRAVURA!

Watching dancers from the Balkans you sometimes get the impression that they are powered by rockets! The Balkans cover a big area, stretching from Yugoslavia to Greece, taking in Albania and Bulgaria on the way, and down the centuries the mountains and plains have seen plenty of action. Invaders and conquerors have passed and some have stayed, so it is hardly surprising that the dances of the people spring from many different races.

Pictured here are Yugoslavians of Opanak, the country's Dance Company. These handsome Yugoslavs are not only tremendously talented and exciting dancers, but are living reminders of the stormy past and more peaceful present of the Balkans. In their dances you can see influences from the Turks, the Hungarians and the Greeks, as well as Serbian, Croatian, Slovenian, Macedonian and Montenegran dances—which sounds rather like a geography lesson, but that is what happens when you start discussing the many racial strands that make up a country in the Balkans.

One of the Company's most famous numbers is Vlasi, a colourful shepherd dance. The artists are clad in sheep's wool vests and capes, and carry crooks, which remind audiences that vast areas of Yugoslavia are still populated by farming folk.

As the pictures show very clearly, apart from the lively routines which the Yugoslavs display, there are

Yugoslav men making their considerable most of one of their big moments. There are plenty more to come!

also lovely costumes to delight the eyes of the spectators. All the very many peoples of the Balkans have colourful national costumes, which really look as if they belong to the wearers, and are not simply garments that are put on for special occasions.

Many tourists have discovered the delights of Balkan dancing, but the people of the Balkans do not keep good things to themselves, and there is always a chance that a troupe may suddenly appear in Western Europe to stir even the staidest audience into a frenzy.

Yugoslav men making their considerable most of one of their big moments. There are plenty more to come!

Below.
The accent is on red and white in this lovely line-up of Balkan beauties.

HAWAIIAN HULA

"Bring on the dancing girls!" That is what the average visitor hopes will happen when he visits the Hawaiian Islands, which are set in the very centre of the mighty Pacific Ocean. And, judging by the pictures on this page, who can blame the average visitor?

There are not that many full-blooded Hawaiians left in the islands, but the old dances—the most famous is the hula, or hula-hula—live on, and so do the famous grass skirts. Hawaii may be the 50th state of the U.S.A. but it remains—in some ways at least—the tropical paradise it has always been. And its lovely dancers nowadays travel the world to entertain enchanted audiences. But they are best seen at home. Has anyone got a spare airline ticket?

GO-GO GIRLS

You've seen them in action in *Top of the Pops.* They are the ones that provide the programme's only real dancing! Pan's People is their name, a talented quintet of girls who bring some real style to the proceedings. Not that we're knocking pop! We wouldn't dream of it! But Pan's People are something special.

They started working together in the late 1960s, and one of the group, Flick Colby, has done the choreography from the beginning, though she no longer actually dances in the group. Europe got to know the girls better than Britain at first, but all that has changed now. Lucky us!

As readers of this book might guess, hours of hard work are put in by the girls before their stunning star spots.

Little charmers from Korea

Let's be honest! When some dance lovers heard about the Little Angels—the National Folk Ballet of Korea—they groaned!

Not that they hated children, of course—in the right place—but to pay out good money to watch a bunch of kids, 29 little girls and 3 boys, seemed a bit daft. However charming and clever they were, surely the whole affair would not have much to do with the Art of Dance!

They are officially called the Little Angels, and no one who has seen them would object.

A group of gorgeous girls!
The audience finds itself
smiling as well!

The Little Angels do
have their own small band,
but now and then everyone
gets into the act.

How wrong their fears turned out to be!
London's first glimpse of the troupe at Sadler's
Wells Theatre in 1971 only confirmed what New
York and Mexico City had felt earlier. "Phenom-
enal!" wrote the New York Times critic, and in
Mexico, where the youngsters performed at the
Arts Festival held alongside the 1968 Olympics,
one writer was so overcome that he wrote: "The
Little Angels wove a spell of Oriental magic which
held the international audience spellbound."

A line-up of the little lovelies!

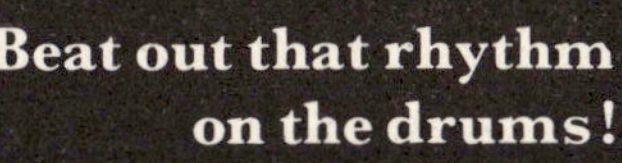

Beat out that rhythm on the drums!

audiences throw flowers.

More drum beats with a smile.

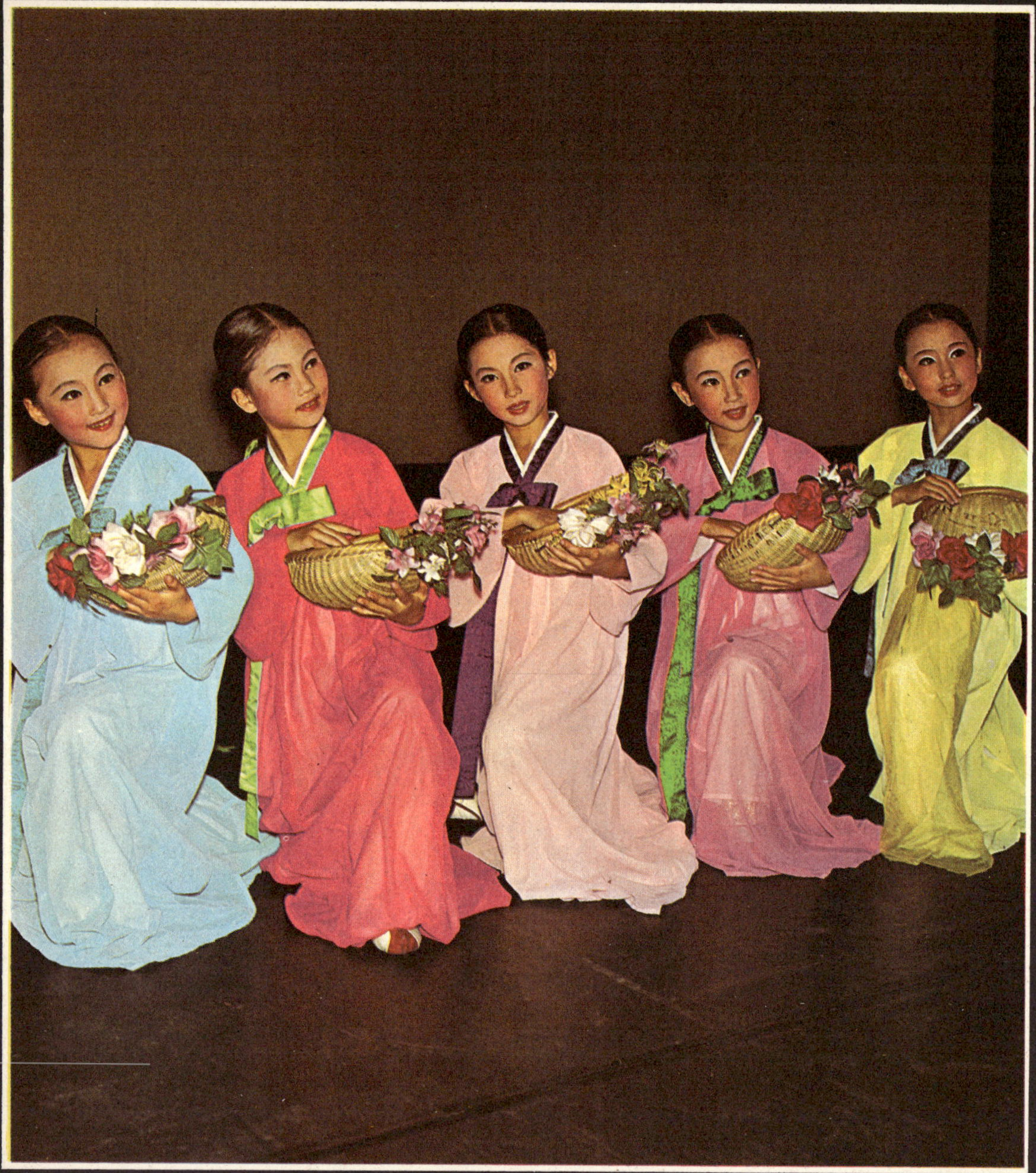

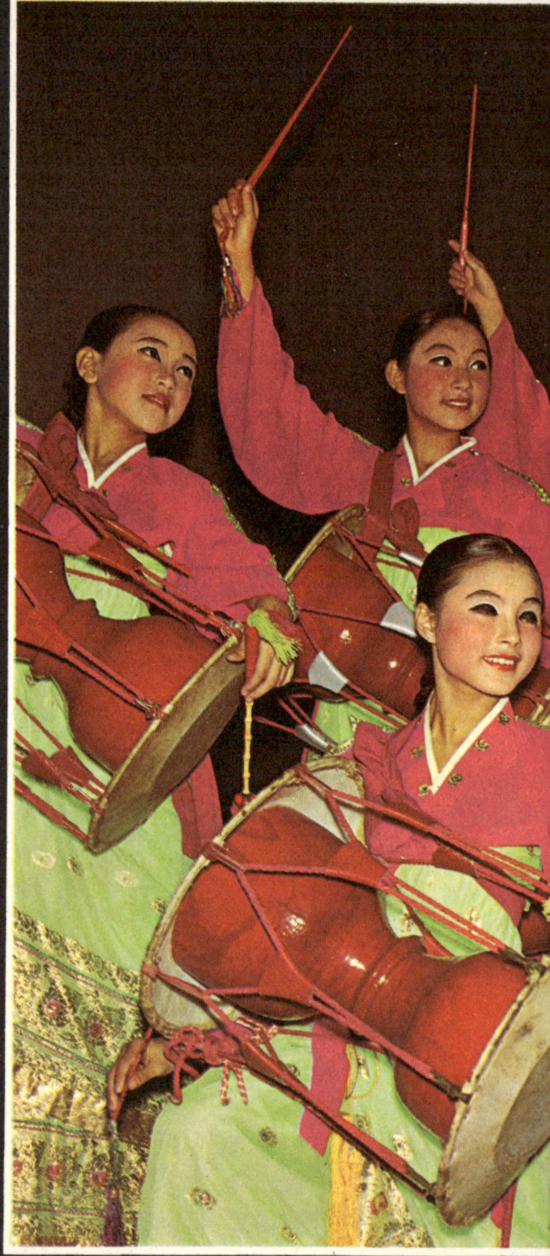

In other words, the kids were the tops!

Korea, on the mainland of Asia opposite Japan, has been a home of dancing for centuries. Koreans revere it, love its beauty and the happiness it brings. Ancient legends and folk stories are used in many of the dances, some of them serious, some plain mischievous.

The Little Angels always have an "Aak", or court music orchestra, which has five grown-up players who have to play fifty different instruments! Those musicians certainly have to be versatile!

The Angels have played before the President of

**And a tug-of-war—
or peace!—at the end.**

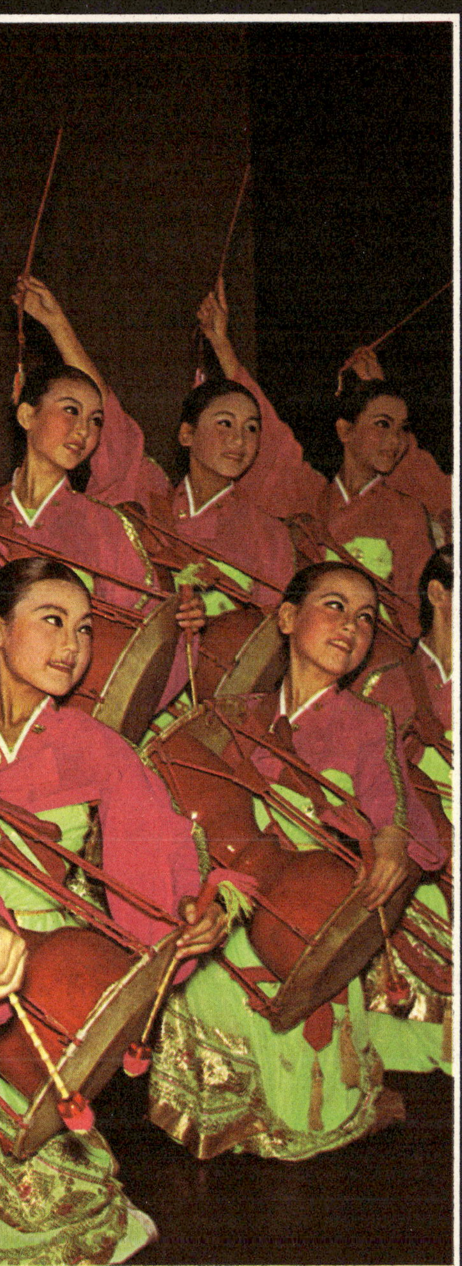

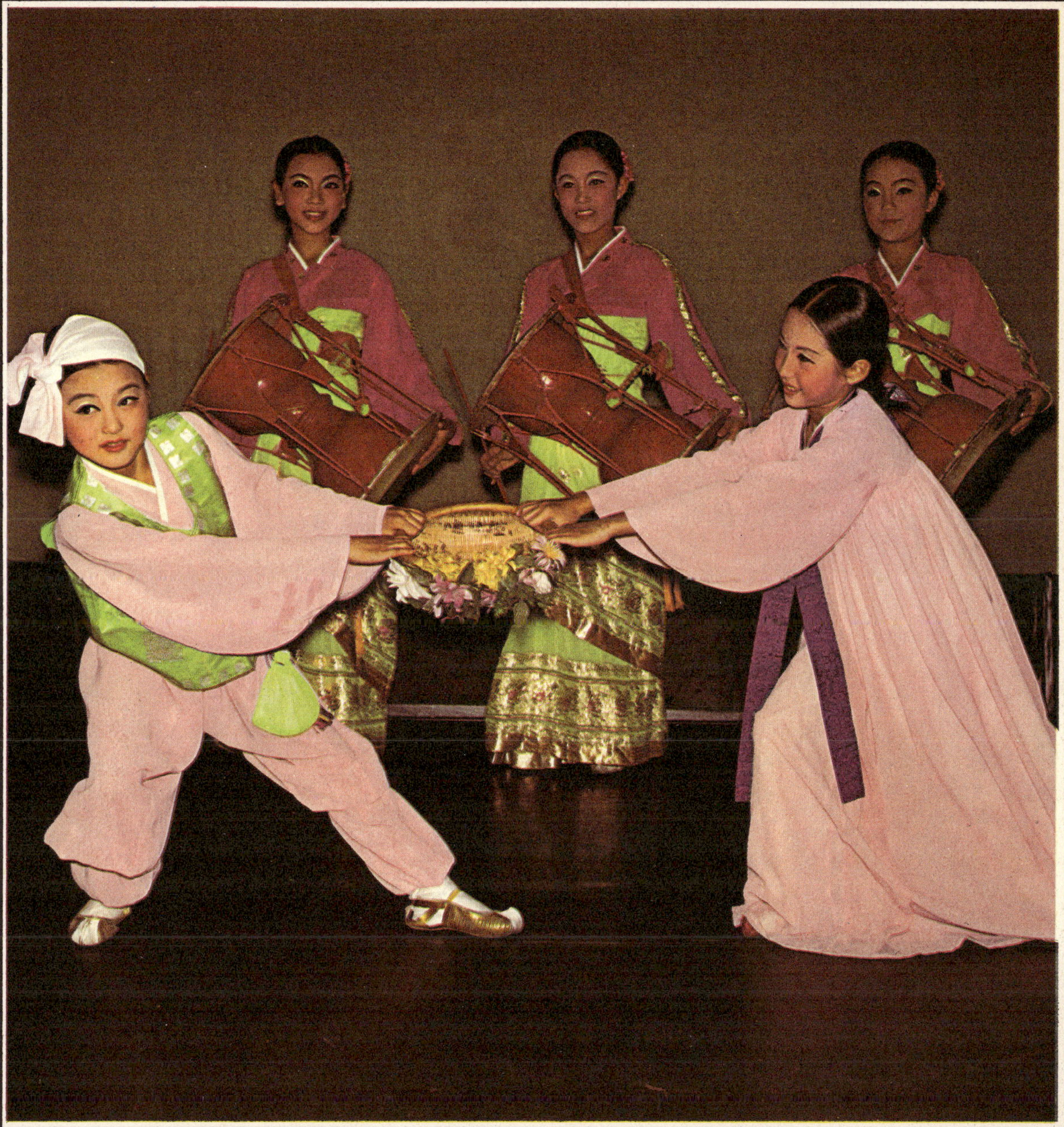

the United States and have appeared in many theatres as well as on TV in America, Britain and elsewhere. Along the way they have brought happiness to millions.

They certainly seem a happy bunch themselves—audiences can guess that simply by looking at their smiles. Those who think that Far Eastern peoples take their pleasures rather seriously, with faces kept firmly straight, should see the Little Angels having a ball!

And not only having a ball, for the dances they do are performed with true artistry, a combination of natural talent and sheer hard work!

INDIAN ENCHANTMENT

Even before Westerners are thrilled by the dancing of the Kathakali Drama Company, they are struck by the amazing make-up and costumes of the troupe—one look at the pictures will show why! All the troupe are males from Kerala in India, which helps explain their fabulous faces, for Kerala means "land of the coconut", and coconut oil is used in their make-up.

The oil is mixed with brilliantly coloured pigments, and, just for the record, if you see a mainly green face you know the character is a "goodie", while if there's a lot of black about him, he's a "baddie"!

Kathakali is a 2,000-year-old temple dance drama, the story being chanted while the cast acts it silently in mime, with plenty of interruptions for dancing, plus loud drum beats to go with it!

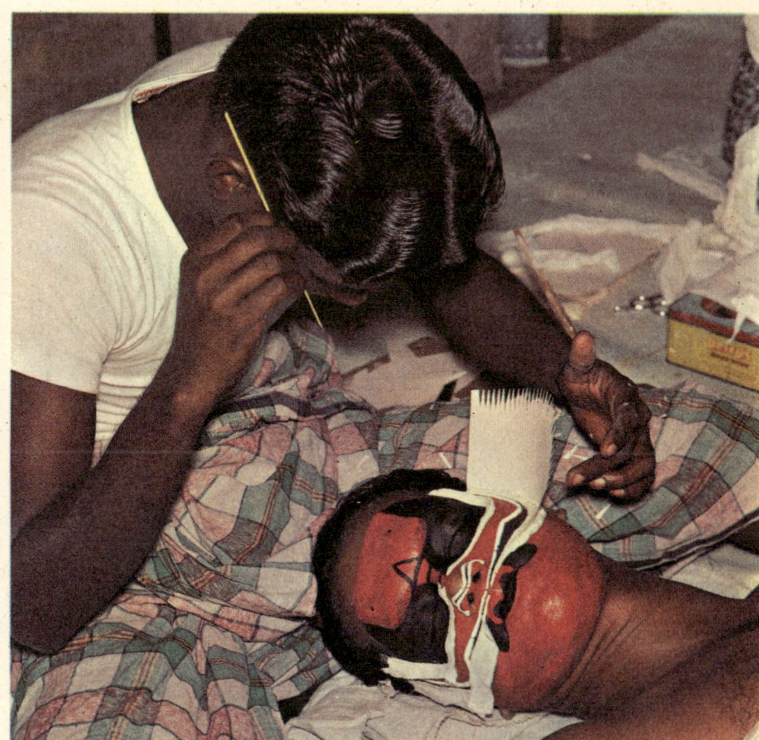

BENGAL WARRIORS

You don't expect to find a brilliant, totally unknown dance troupe on a country ramble, but that is what happened to Professor Bhattacharya of Calcutta University in India.

Back in 1961, he was wandering around Bengal collecting local folk songs, when someone advised him to call at a village in Purulia 50 miles from the nearest railway station. There he found the Chhau dancers and became their patron.

The dancers, men who performed every year before their crops were put in, were in a bad way, and their splendid masks were, too. But all that has changed now, thanks to the Professor, who got the authorities in the capital Delhi interested, and thanks also to a lady called Milena Salvini.

Now these striking and exciting dancers from Bengal have become used to performing publicly, not only in India far from their native Chhau villages, but in Europe as well. But they still work on the land when they are not dancing. Their area is a very poor one, and the money they bring back from their tours helps their families enjoy a better life.

Londoners had a chance to see the Chhau Dancers in 1972, when they appeared at the Sadler's Wells Theatre. You could say that their story was a real life fairy tale, couldn't you?

Don't be fooled by some of the masks you see in these pictures of Bengal's Chhau Dancers—all the performers are men. Nobody knows how old some of their dances are. They may go back several thousand years to ancient hunting rites before the warriors of the tribe went out to seek food. What is certain is that for sheer colour, zest and glamour, these dancers, totally unknown to the outside world a few years ago, have caught the public's fancy in a big way.

Graceful JAPANESE RITUALS

Imagine going to the theatre and finding yourself watching a colourful mixture of high jinks, dismal tragedy, song, dance, speech and spectacle. It sounds a splendid hotch-potch, doesn't it?

If you have the luck to visit Japan, you will be able to enjoy all these different things rolled into one in the Kabuki theatre, over 400 years old and still going strong.

Like much of Japanese life, Kabuki is a sort of organised ritual, but, oddly, it is also an anti-ritual! It was invented by a woman around 1600, though now only men perform it. Japanese theatre had got rather stodgy at that time, plays called "No" being so full of ritual that many people thought a bright change was badly needed. "No" plays have survived to this day, but they are not so popular as Kabuki.

Considering that a woman invented the new art, it seems a bit hard that men now have all the action! But what happened back in the 1600s was that the entertainments got rather naughty, and the Government decided that a naughty all-male show was better than a naughty all-female one! Unfair to girls, perhaps, but that's show business!

So all-boy Kabuki replaced the all-girl ones. And they *were* boys at first, though now all the performers, like those in the pictures, are men, including those playing female parts.

When Kabuki visits the West, the performances are shortened. Just as well, perhaps, for back home they tend to last about five hours. A stranger not knowing what was going on, might find that rather long!

Not that the Japanese are above the odd nap during a performance, or a quick trip to the shops to collect the groceries. The great thing is for everyone to enjoy themselves, to have a nice, relaxing time.

And even if you don't know what is going on at a Kabuki show, there is still plenty to see. The accent is on spectacle, lovely costumes, lovely scenery—lots of it—and plenty of audience participation. If you feel like cheering the villain, or jeering him, feel free to do so! And nowadays, back in Japan at least, modern machinery allows whole dance troupes plus an orchestra to come up on lifts through trap-doors and start entertaining everyone. That old Japanese magic works wonders!

Gaiety from Guinea

Look at a map of Africa, and from its western tip at Cape Verde southwards to where the mighty River Congo flows into the Atlantic is the Guinea Coast. Now that coast, and the interior behind it, is divided up into many nations. But one thing nearly all of them have in common is a love of dancing.

Nowadays, when the Dance has become an international art, many companies have left Africa to display their skills and colourful rhythms over-seas, like those in the pictures from Sierra Leone. West Africa has had a stormy history, so not all the dances are gay. Some are about wars and battles long ago, others about the terrible slave trade which resulted in millions of Africans being shipped as slaves to the West Indies and America from the 16th to the 19th century, a dreadful blot on the European nations who ran the trade. But most of the dances express the typical African joy of life, the feeling that happiness is the object of existence, not gloom.

And many of the dances are concerned with magic and tribal ritual, and about dramas that happened to the ancestors of the performers. You can expect a bit of everything when you watch those dancers from Guinea!

Romeo and Juliet

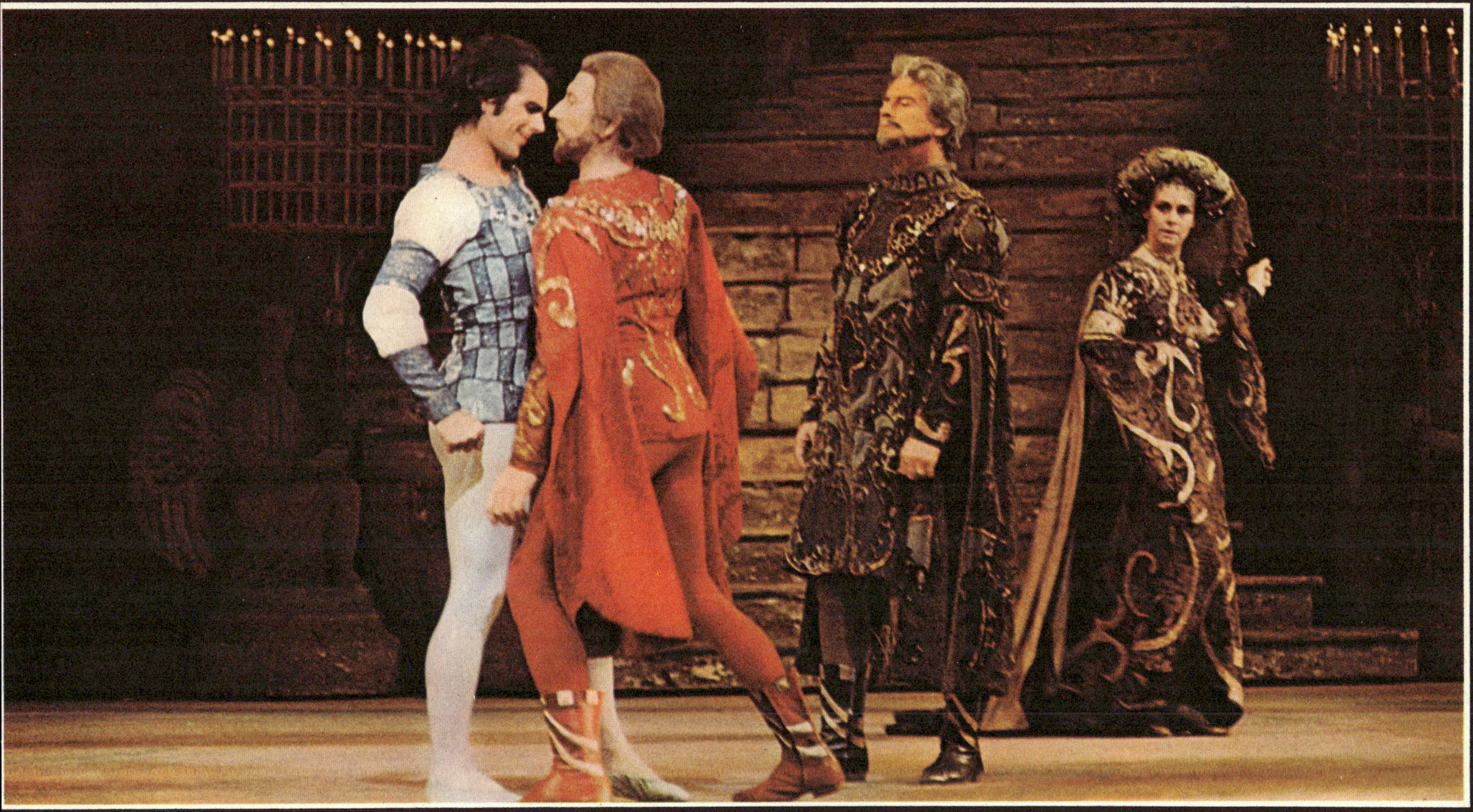

The great Russian composer, Serge Prokofiev, must have sometimes wondered if he would ever see his Romeo and Juliet staged! First the Kirov Theatre, Leningrad, suggested a ballet based on Shakespeare's immortal love story, then they turned it down, then Moscow's Bolshoi Theatre insultingly said that the music was unsuitable for dancing!

After other setbacks, it was first performed in 1938 in Czechoslovakia, but Leningrad at last came to its senses and gave it with choreography by the brilliant dancer, Leonide Lavrovsky.

Even then there was trouble. "We can't hear the music," complained the ballerina at one point in rehearsals, but finally, in 1940, the ballet opened to wild applause. Since then it has gone into the repertoire of many great companies including London's Royal Ballet.

The ballet is set in the ancient Italian city of Verona where two great families, the Capulets and the Montagues, hate each other so much that they are continually fighting in the streets. After a fierce fight at the beginning of the ballet, the Prince of Verona orders them to end their feud.

All the pictures of *Romeo and Juliet* in these pages come from Kenneth McMillan's famous production for the Royal Ballet, using Prokofiev's great score.

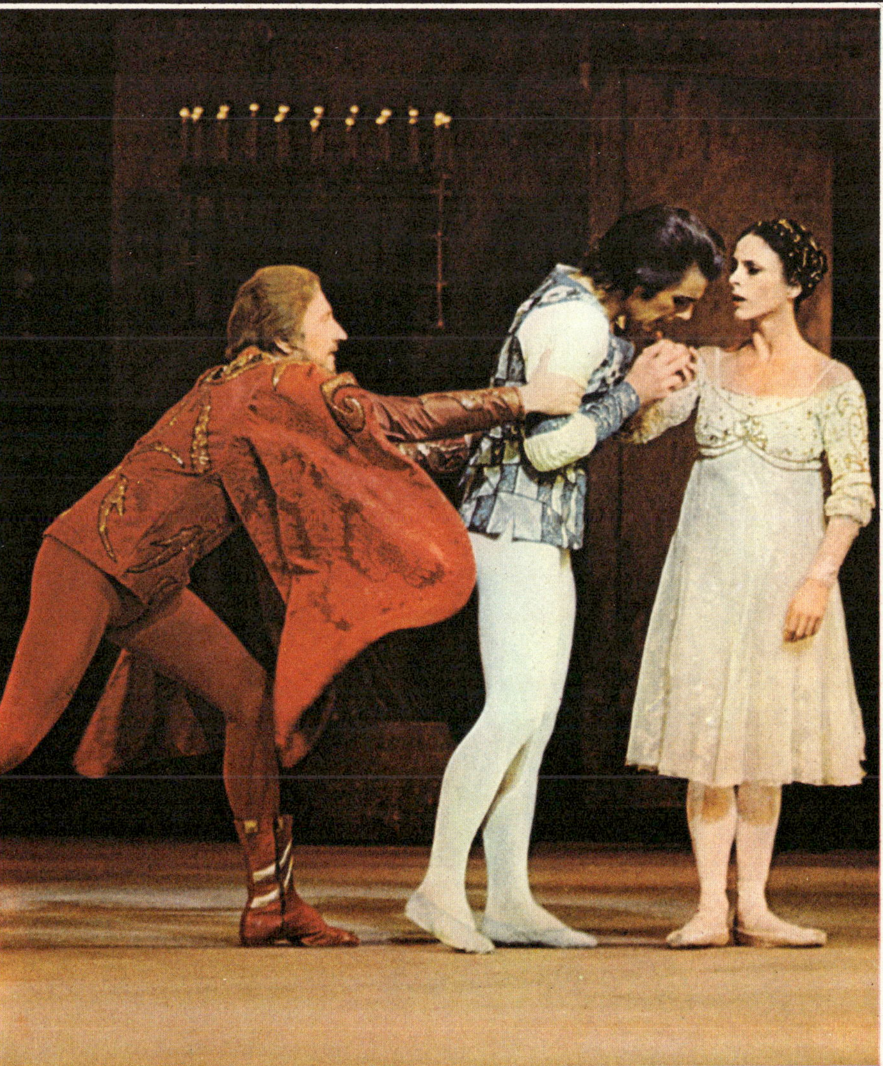

In the centre of this picture is Friar Laurence, who plays a key part in the action.

One of the spectacular fights, which play such a thrilling part in this ballet.

There is plenty of time for enjoyment between tragic moments.

One of the supreme highlights
of ballet is the death of
Romeo's friend Mercutio in a
duel with Tybalt, Juliet's fiery
cousin. Romeo later revenges
his friend's death.

Juliet, the daughter of Lord Capulet, meets Romeo, Montague's handsome son, at a masked ball in her house, only to discover that they should be deadly enemies!

That night Juliet, unable to sleep, wanders onto her balcony and sees Romeo below. They declare their love for each other.

The pair are secretly married by a Friar Laurence, but then disaster strikes. Romeo is in Verona's main square with his friend Mercutio, when Juliet's fiery cousin, Tybalt, challenges him to fight. He refuses because of his love for Juliet, and Mercutio takes Tybalt on, only to be run through when Romeo tries to part them. The enraged Romeo kills Tybalt then is forced to flee and is banished in his absence.

He spends his wedding night secretly with Juliet, then flees to the city of Mantua. Juliet meanwhile is ordered by her father to marry a Count Paris. To help her, the Friar gives her a potion to make her seem dead and she is put in the tomb of her family to await Romeo's return. But he hears she is really dead, comes back, finds her, and kills himself. She awakes, sees him, and kills herself, too. The heartbroken Capulets and Montagues end their feud—too late!

Highspots of *Romeo
and Juliet* include
beautiful dances for
the two young
lovers, especially
those on their
wedding night.

Fascinating Filipinos

Lying between the Pacific and the China Seas are the Philippine Islands, over 7,000 of them, and many of them romantic and exciting. So it is not surprising that the Islands have produced a dance troupe, the Bayhanihan-Philippino Folk Dance Company, which has thrilled dance lovers everywhere. Filipinos are naturally graceful, but the members of the troupe, begun under the wing of the Women's University of Manila in the 1950s, are more than graceful—they are brilliant! They present every kind of dance from ancient native rituals to Spanish dances—Spain once owned the Philippines. Music and costumes are splendid, and from the outset things went with a swing because the dance director, Lucrezia Urtilla, was so superb.

Some folk dance companies present a very narrow range of dances. Not so the fabulous Filipinos, whose lovely routines span many centuries of the Islands' history. As the pictures show. Eastern magic is at work.

Brazilian Rhythm

"I've got rhythm !'' could be the motto of every Brazilian boy and girl ! They seem to be born dancers. Believe it or not, many of Brazil's best professional dancers are self-taught.

Add to this natural skill the beat of the drums and stunning costumes and the result is a riot of movement, colour and excitement.

The pictures on these and the following pages are of the Brasiliana company of Rio de Janeiro, the romantic, fabulous capital of Brazil until the new city of Brasilia took its place. Many of the dances are inspired by South American folklore, but the actual dancing is very much influenced by the great Rio Carnival when the city is given over to mass enjoyment.

The company has around 40 dancers, and their musicians play strange sounding instruments with even stranger names—ouica, caxixi, agogo and so on. The dances are Sambas, Bossa Novas, Frevos, Marchas, Boyon, Chorros and other exotic, exciting numbers. Rio's Carnival goes on for days and is enjoyed by Brazilians and tourists alike. The Brasiliana company seem to sum up all the spirit of the Carnival in an hour or two of electrifying, joyous excitement.

The famous Bossa Nova, one of their most popular dances was once called the Bossa Vecha. Its origins date back to earlier times when there was general rejoicing after sailors had returned safely home. In fact, many South American carnivals date back to similar sorts of event—men returning from the wars and so on.

The only trouble about the Brasiliana company is that it tends to make other similar companies seem pale by comparison! And on top of everything else, those native rhythms seem almost to have a hypnotic effect on audiences. What a wonderful way to be hypnotised!

Swan Lake

Only half this lovely ballet is set by the lake and our pictures show the other half, full of vivid colours, gaiety, dancing and romance.

The wonder is that this ever popular romantic ballet survived its first performance!

The music by the great Tchaikovsky was marvellous, the story was good, but everything else was appalling! The choreographer—the man who had invented the steps and staged the work—was a dud, and so was the conductor, who was also a butcher: not being very good at reading music (!), he changed some of Tchaikovsky's for someone else's, which was easier!

As for the scenery, it had been used before—and looked it—while the ballerina was yet another second-rater. So it was not surprisingly that the first performance, at Moscow's Bolshoi Theatre in 1877, was a flop. Fortunately, it was successfully revived at St. Petersburg, now Leningrad, in 1895, and has been adored ever since.

The hero of the story is Prince Siegfried, who, at a party to celebrate his coming-of-age, is reminded by his stern mother that he must choose a bride at the next Court Ball.